everyday
STEM

SCIENCE

SPACE

Science is all around you!

KINGFISHER
LONDON & NEW YORK

First published 2023 in the United States
by Kingfisher
120 Broadway, New York, NY 10271
Kingfisher is an imprint of
Macmillan Children's Books, London
All rights reserved.

Copyright © Macmillan Publishers
International Ltd 2023

ISBN 978-0-7534-7848-6

Distributed in the U.S. and Canada by Macmillan,
120 Broadway, New York, NY 10271

Library of Congress Cataloging-in-Publication data has been applied for.

Author: Izzie Clarke
Illustrator: James Lancett
Series editor: Lizzie Davey
Series design: Jim Green

Kingfisher Books are available for special promotions and premiums.
For details contact:
Special Markets Department, Macmillan
120 Broadway, New York, NY 10271.

For more information please visit:
www.kingfisherbooks.com

Printed in China
2 4 6 8 9 7 5 3 1
1TR/1122/UG/WKT/128MA

EU representative: 1st Floor, The Liffey Trust Centre
117-126 Sheriff Street Upper, Dublin 1 D01 YC43

FSC
www.fsc.org

MIX
Paper | Supporting
responsible forestry
FSC® C116313

CONTENTS

WHAT IS SPACE?

We often refer to the vast, expanding universe as "space." Space begins at the outer edge of our planet and goes on forever. What we do know is that it's a vacuum, which means there's no air to scatter noise or light. However, space contains many wonders. Planets are born from clouds of dust and gas, along with dazzling stars and swirling galaxies. And we can't forget the puzzling supermassive black holes and the mysterious invisible forces that hold everything together!

EARTH

Our home, Earth, is the fifth-largest planet in our solar system. Outer space "starts" at around 62 mi. (100 km) above sea level.

THE SOLAR SYSTEM

Eight planets orbit our star, the Sun. Together, they form our solar system. On average, there are 2.8 billion mi. (4.5 billion km) between the Sun and the outermost planet, Neptune.

THE MILKY WAY

Our solar system is positioned in in a galaxy called the Milky Way, which contains around 100 billion stars.

DARK ENERGY & DARK MATTER

We don't actually know what most of the universe is made of. However, astronomers study invisible influences that impact how galaxies and stars move. It's a bit like how you can't see the wind, but you can see trees swaying as it blows.

One thing that astronomers can see is that distant galaxies are moving away from us. But why? Scientists think it's because of an invisible force called dark energy. There is also invisible stuff that has enough gravity to pull on stars and galaxies—this is called dark matter.

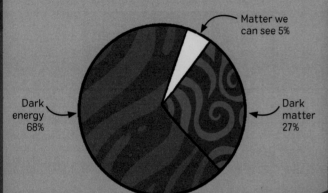

Matter we can see 5%

Dark energy 68%

Dark matter 27%

THE UNIVERSE

The universe is made of all the stars, planets, galaxies, dust, and everything else. It is 13.7 billion years old. We can see the "echo" of its creation in something called the cosmic microwave background.

SUPERCLUSTERS

Superclusters are the largest structures in the universe. Each supercluster contains a number of groups of galaxies and can spread over several million light-years.

5

GRAVITY

Gravity is an important force that exists everywhere across space and in our daily lives. Put simply, it's the pull between two objects. It's thanks to gravity that you don't drift off into space every time you jump, that the Moon orbits Earth, and that Earth orbits the Sun. This all comes down to "mass"—how much matter an object is made of. The bigger the mass, the bigger the gravitational pull. In fact, you exert a gravitational force on Earth in the same way that it does on you. However, Earth is much more "massive" than you, which means your force doesn't affect the planet to the same extent.

APPLE ON THE MOVE

The story goes that British mathematician Sir Isaac Newton came up with his law of gravity after seeing an apple fall from a tree. He realized that something had to be acting on falling objects; otherwise, they would stay still. That something is a force—gravity.

WEIGHT AND MASS

Your **mass** always stays the same and is measured in kilograms by scientists. However, the amount you weigh can change depending on where you are in the universe, because **weight** is a measure of the force of gravity that's acting on you. Weight is measured in Newtons.

Weight (N) = Mass (kg) x Gravitational Acceleration (m/s²)

On **Earth** the gravitational acceleration is 9.8 m/s².

On the **Moon** the gravitational acceleration is 1.6 m/s², which means you'd weigh a sixth of your Earth weight.

ESCAPE VELOCITY

An "escape velocity" is the speed at which something can overcome Earth's gravity. To leave the planet, rockets (or even a very fast football) would need to travel at 7 mi. (11.2 km) per second.

BLACK HOLES

The most massive things in the universe are black holes. Another famous scientist, Albert Einstein, explained that the gravitational pull from these objects is so strong that nothing can escape from them, not even light!

NICOLAUS COPERNICUS
(1473-1543)

In the 1500s, it was strongly believed that Earth was the center of everything. That was until a Polish astronomer, Nicolaus Copernicus, observed the motion of Mercury, Mars, Jupiter, and Saturn. He figured out that the planets in fact revolve around the Sun. His model of the solar system wasn't very popular at the time, but it became fundamental to what we know about planets today.

SEEING SPACE

There are many stars and galaxies in the universe. We can see some of them at night thanks to the light they emit. However, they also send out hidden rays of energy that the naked eye can't detect. These invisible waves are called radiation. Scientists categorize the different types of radiation on an important scale called the electromagnetic spectrum.

THE ELECTROMAGNETIC SPECTRUM

The electromagnetic spectrum helps scientists "see" astronomical objects and has uses on Earth too. Phones, TVs, and radios use radio waves. These also help astronomers study galaxies. We use X-rays to photograph broken bones, as well as to study black holes.

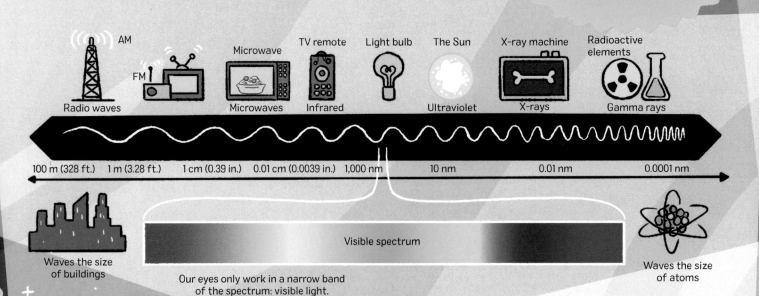

AM
FM
Radio waves

Microwave
Microwaves

TV remote
Infrared

Light bulb

The Sun
Ultraviolet

X-ray machine
X-rays

Radioactive elements
Gamma rays

| 100 m (328 ft.) | 1 m (3.28 ft.) | 1 cm (0.39 in.) | 0.01 cm (0.0039 in.) | 1,000 nm | 10 nm | 0.01 nm | 0.0001 nm |

Waves the size of buildings

Visible spectrum

Waves the size of atoms

Our eyes only work in a narrow band of the spectrum: visible light.

THE DOPPLER EFFECT

Sound, like radiation, travels in waves. An ambulance siren will sound different when it's traveling toward you or away from you. Similarly, radiation from an object moving toward or away from us sends different signals. We call this change in frequency the Doppler effect.

TELESCOPES AND TIME TRAVELING

Observing light from distant galaxies and stars is like time traveling. Light has to travel millions of miles, which means when it finally reaches us, we're actually seeing light from the past. If we observe a galaxy 5,000 light-years away, that means we're seeing what it looked like 5,000 years ago.

GRAVITATIONAL LENSING

Light usually travels in a straight line. However, gravity from massive objects can be so heavy that it distorts space and causes the path of light to bend and curve. This is known as gravitational lensing.

Refracting and reflecting telescopes

Telescopes are designed to detect different forms of radiation. There are two types that use visible light:

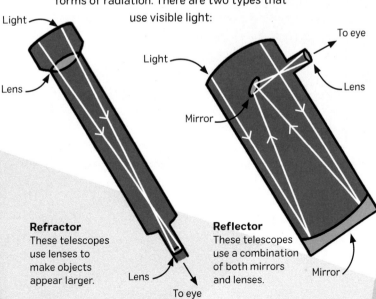

Light
Lens

Light
To eye
Lens
Mirror

Refractor
These telescopes use lenses to make objects appear larger.

Lens
To eye

Reflector
These telescopes use a combination of both mirrors and lenses.

Mirror

STAR STUFF

Almost everything we know can be traced back to "star stuff." Stars are made of very hot gas that burns over their lifetime. When the very first stars used all their gas, they died in spectacular stellar explosions, flinging everything they were made of across the universe. This life cycle repeated time and time again, creating the building blocks for new life. It formed new generations of stars, new worlds, and—after a very long time—it even created us!

BIG BANG

The universe began 13.7 billion years ago with an event called the big bang. It created the important elements hydrogen and helium and a tiny amount of lithium.

STARS

The first stars after the big bang were huge! They used hydrogen and helium as fuel and eventually created new, slightly heavier elements.

SUPERNOVAS

Once all of a star's fuel is used up, it starts to die. Massive stars end their lives in a stunning stellar explosion called a supernova. During these explosions, heavier elements were thrown into space and made up the next generation of stars.

SPLITTING LIGHT

Light can be split up into different frequencies, which create different colors. This is what happens when you pass light through a prism, or when sunlight travels through droplets of water to create a rainbow.

Hydrogen

Each element interacts with light in its own unique way. Scientists study light patterns from distant galaxies, planets, or clouds of dust and compare them with patterns from known elements to figure out what they're made of.

ARE THE RIGHT ELEMENTS OUT THERE?

Astrobiologists are always looking for the right conditions for life on other planets. That includes a good temperature, liquid water, and signs of oxygen. In 2015, NASA's Cassini mission found water on Saturn's moon Enceladus: giant jets of water vapor and liquid oceans beneath an icy crust.

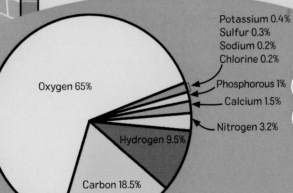

ELEMENTS FOUND IN THE HUMAN BODY

Potassium 0.4%
Sulfur 0.3%
Sodium 0.2%
Chlorine 0.2%

Phosphorous 1%
Calcium 1.5%
Nitrogen 3.2%

Oxygen 65%
Hydrogen 9.5%
Carbon 18.5%

REPEAT

This process was repeated over generations, creating even heavier elements that are found throughout space, in planets, on Earth, and even in the human body.

YOU

American astronomer Carl Sagan said that "we're made of star stuff." What he meant was that almost all of the elements found in the human body were originally made in stars.

SPACE ROCKS!

Our planet is 4.5 billion years old. We know that thanks to an area of science called geology, which is the study of rocks. Ancient rocks can act as a time capsule, revealing what Earth was like millions of years ago, how hot it would have been, and the strength of its important magnetic field. But there are still a lot of big questions about our solar system. Are the answers hiding in space rocks?

Volcanoes
On Earth, volcanoes form as a result of plate tectonics—huge chunks of Earth's surface moving around.

DUST CLOUD
Planets form when clouds of dust and rocks are pulled together by a star's gravity.

Craters
Craters are left when a meteorite lands on Earth. Most have been wiped off the surface due to tectonic activity.

EARTH
Studying planet Earth helps us figure out mysteries about our rocky neighboring planets and asteroids within the solar system.

Rocks on the move
Rocks and dust can be moved to different locations by storms, gravity, ice, and water.

EARTH'S MOON

Moon rock
Samples of Moon rock have been collected by Apollo astronauts, Russian rovers, and most recently China's Chang'e 5.

Ceres
This dwarf planet has a radius of 296 mi. (476 km) and is the largest object in the asteroid belt.

Craters
Craters on the Moon show us that it was once a violent place, frequently hit by space rocks.

Seas
The dark patches on the Moon are marks left from ancient volcanic eruptions. They are known as "seas."

MARS

For the first time ever, robots are going to collect rock samples from Mars and return them to Earth. Planetary geologists will study them in the hope of finding out if there was once life on Mars.

GALILEO GALILEI (1564–1642)

Galileo was an Italian astronomer. He invented a powerful telescope lens and was the first to observe the rings of Saturn, the different phases of Venus, and the moons of Jupiter. Seeing these moons orbit another planet proved that Earth was not the center of the universe, as was thought at the time. Galileo proved that Copernicus was right—that the Sun was the center of our solar system. This controversial discovery went against the beliefs of the Catholic Church at the time, and Galileo spent the rest of his life under house arrest.

THE SOLAR SYSTEM

Building the solar system we know today was no easy job. Like a lot of things in space, the Sun was born out of a dense cloud of gas and dust, 4.5 billion years ago. The planets came along after rocks collided and clumped together with the force of the Sun's gravity. Any small leftovers from this turbulent time formed the moons, asteroids, and dwarf planets that are scattered across the solar system.

THE SUN

Earth
Ours is the only planet in the universe known to host life—so far!

Mars
This is known as the "Red Planet" because of its surface, but it has blue sunsets.

Mercury
This is the closest planet to the Sun and also the smallest. It is only slightly bigger than Earth's moon.

Venus
A toxic atmosphere makes Venus hotter than Mercury even though it is farther away from the Sun.

ROCKY PLANETS

These four planets are closest to the Sun. They are made of rock and metal and have hard surfaces. Like Earth, each rocky planet is divided into layers. At the center is a metal core. Then comes a rocky silicate layer called the mantle, and finally the crust, which is the layer we can see.

DID YOU KNOW?

Spacecraft have visited every planet in our solar system.

The asteroid belt
This is a band of ancient space rubble. There's enough space between the pieces for spacecraft to travel through.

YOUR SPACE AGE

It takes Earth 365 days (one Earth year) to travel around the Sun. Other planets make the same journey, but not in the same number of days. So how many years old would you be on other planets?

$$\text{Your space age} = \frac{\text{Your age} \times 365}{\text{Planet year}}$$

Mercury year	88 Earth days
Venus year	225 Earth days
Earth year	365 Earth days
Mars year	687 Earth days
Jupiter year	4,333 Earth days
Saturn year	10,759 Earth days
Uranus year	30,687 Earth days
Neptune year	60,190 Earth days

DID YOU KNOW?

Pluto was once thought of as a planet, but it was demoted to dwarf planet status in 2006. Except for Ceres, other dwarf planets can be found in the Kuiper Belt, which is at the end of our solar system, after the gas giants.

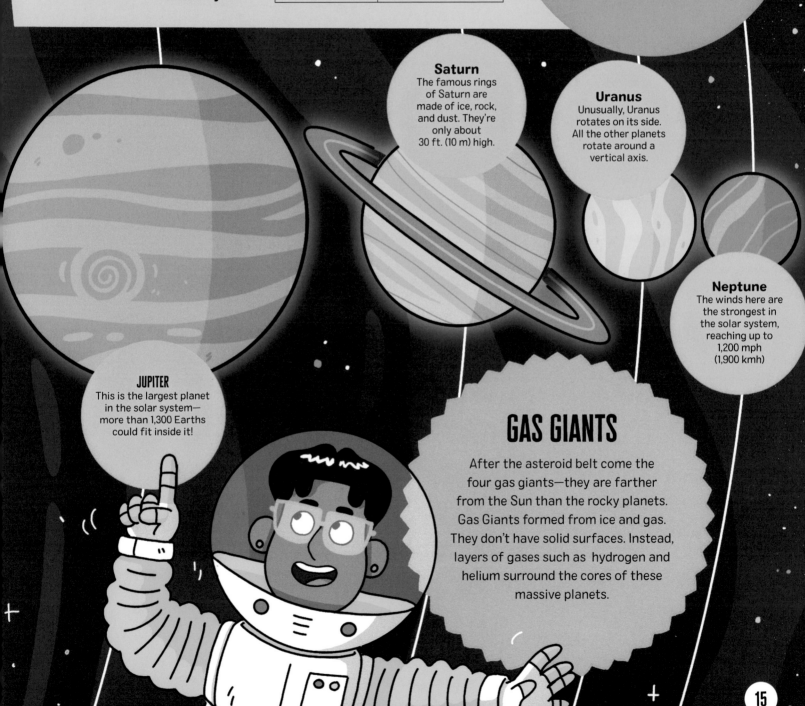

Saturn
The famous rings of Saturn are made of ice, rock, and dust. They're only about 30 ft. (10 m) high.

Uranus
Unusually, Uranus rotates on its side. All the other planets rotate around a vertical axis.

Neptune
The winds here are the strongest in the solar system, reaching up to 1,200 mph (1,900 kmh)

JUPITER
This is the largest planet in the solar system—more than 1,300 Earths could fit inside it!

GAS GIANTS

After the asteroid belt come the four gas giants—they are farther from the Sun than the rocky planets. Gas Giants formed from ice and gas. They don't have solid surfaces. Instead, layers of gases such as hydrogen and helium surround the cores of these massive planets.

THE SUN

We owe a lot to the Sun. Without it, Earth would be an ice-coated rock, and we certainly wouldn't be here. The Sun is our local star. It is made of hydrogen and helium and, on average, is about 93 million mi. (150 million km) away. The hottest part of the Sun is its core, which can reach a whopping 27 million °F (15 million °C). Large explosions can take place on its surface that are so energetic that highly charged particles, called plasma, escape the Sun's gravity. This stream of particles is called the "solar wind."

INSIDE THE SUN

The Sun is divided into layers that all drive different processes. The four key layers are the core at the center, then the radiation zone, then the convection zone, then the corona at the Sun's surface.

Corona

Convection zone

Radiation zone

Core

WARNING!

Never look directly at the Sun

NUCLEAR FUSION

In the Sun's core, hydrogen particles smash together to create helium in a process known as nuclear fusion. Scientists are trying to re-create this process on Earth, which could create almost endless electricity. However, it's difficult to build a mini star in a laboratory because of the high temperatures and pressures needed.

Cold water sinks

Warm water rises

Heat

CONVECTION

When we heat a pan of water, the hot water rises to the surface then cools and sinks to the bottom. This is called convection. The same process happens in the Sun's convection zone. Hot plasma rises from the core to the surface, cools, and then sinks back down. This movement produces huge electrical currents and strong magnetic fields.

What does the Sun do on Earth?

Ocean currents
The Sun drives ocean currents. Warm water has more energy to move to different areas, and colder water rushes in to replace it.

Colorful skies
When the solar wind hits Earth's magnetic shield, it creates colorful lights dancing across the sky—the aurora borealis and aurora australis.

Life-giving sunshine
Plants convert sunlight into energy and oxygen. Humans and other animals eat the plants and breathe in the oxygen.

PARKER SOLAR PROBE
Weirdly, the outer edge of the Sun, called the corona, is hotter than its surface. NASA has sent the Parker Solar Probe to fly into the area—closer than we've ever been before—to find out more.

CECELIA PAYNE-GAPOSCHKIN (1900–1979)

Cecelia Payne-Gaposchkin was a groundbreaking astrophysicist—a scientist who applies the laws of physics to space. She used glass plates to capture the Sun's spectrum and discovered that stars are mostly made of hydrogen and helium. Her thesis on stellar atmospheres was published in 1925, and she became the first female professor at Harvard University in 1956.

THE MOON

The Moon is Earth's nearest neighbor, orbiting our planet at an average of 239,000 mi. (385,000 km) away. How the Moon formed has puzzled astronomers for years, but it's thought that it was created 4.5 billion years ago when a small, rocky planet collided with Earth, and the debris from the collision collected in Earth's orbit to form the Moon. Stargazers don't even need a telescope to see the history etched on the Moon's surface. The dark spots, known as maria or "seas," are from ancient volcanic activity, and the lighter patches show where asteroids and comets have pelted its crust.

TIDAL FORCE

The Moon's gravity pulls on Earth's oceans and causes water to bulge in the direction of our rocky neighbor. This creates a high tide. But this tidal force also squeezes the planet slightly, causing a bulge on the other side of the planet. As we rotate, we rotate through these watery bulges to give us two high tides a day.

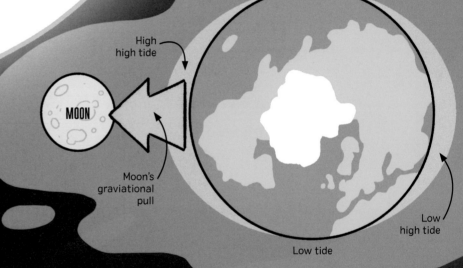

Low tide

High high tide

MOON

Moon's graviational pull

Low high tide

Low tide

PHASES OF THE MOON

The Moon is constantly moving around Earth, but we always see the same side. That's because it spins in a similar amount of time it takes to orbit our blue planet. It looks like the Moon changes shape because the amount lit up by the Sun differs every night.

Northern Hemisphere view

| New moon | Waxing crescent | First quarter | Waxing gibbous | Full moon | Waning gibbous | Last quarter | Waning crescent |

Southern Hemisphere view

| New moon | Waxing crescent | First quarter | Waxing gibbous | Full moon | Waning gibbous | Last quarter | Waning crescent |

FUTURE MISSIONS

China is currently exploring the shadowy, far side of the Moon. Their Chang'e 6 lander will collect samples on the lunar South Pole, and Chang'e 7 will study its rocks, hunt for frozen water, and investigate where the water came from. That might even explain the Moon's mysterious formation. India's Chandrayaan-3 mission will also look for ice and minerals that could be helpful to humans.

Will we return? NASA plans to send the first woman and first person of color to the Moon in the next decade. And the European Space Agency wants to build a lunar village.

MOONWALKERS

Just 12 people have walked on the Moon, and it is the only place in space where humans have set foot. The first astronauts to visit were NASA's Neil Armstrong and Buzz Aldrin on Apollo 11 in July 1969, but no one has been back since 1972. We can still see where astronauts have stomped on the Moon because there's no wind or liquid water to erode their footprints. New prints will be made when humans from NASA's Artemis missions go to the Moon, no earlier than 2025.

EXPLORING OUR SOLAR SYSTEM

There are a lot of unknowns when it comes to our solar system. To explore, it's safer to send machines into space rather than humans. Space agencies such as NASA spend years carefully designing missions to reach mysterious parts of our solar system. Different spacecraft perform different roles: flyby craft travel past a planet, collecting data as they go. Orbiters are pulled in by the planet's gravity and stay a while. There are also spacecraft that journey to the surface of a planet, such as landers or rovers.

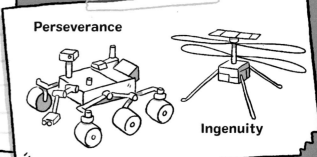

Perseverance

Ingenuity

MISSIONS

So far, Mars is the only planet that has ever had rovers on its surface. NASA's rovers Curiosity and Perseverance are looking for ancient signs of life. Mars is also currently host to a small helicopter, Ingenuity, which can be controlled from Earth. China's first orbiter to the red planet, Tianwen-1, is looking for pockets of water, and the Emirate's Hope Probe will study the Martian atmosphere.

MARS

Mars is a cold, desert-like planet with a thin atmosphere. Its surface appears red because of iron minerals in the soil. Billions of years ago, Mars would have been warmer, and it once supported liquid water.

FEATURES

• **Water**—Rivers, oceans, and lakes were once abundant on Mars. Now the only signs of water are locked away in the planet's icy polar caps.

• **Valleys**—Valles Marineris runs along the equator of Mars. It's 2,500 mi. (4,000 km) long and up to 4 mi. (7 km) deep. For comparison, the average depth of Earth's Grand Canyon is 1 mi. (1.6 km).

• **Volcanoes**—The Martian volcano Olympus Mons is the biggest volcano in our solar system. It is 16 mi. (25 km) high—two and a half times the height of Mount Everest.

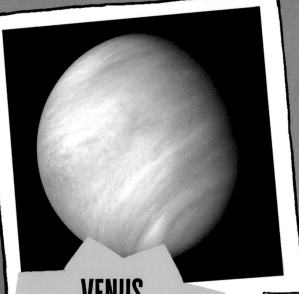

VENUS

Venus has a thick, toxic atmosphere made of carbon dioxide and yellowish clouds of sulfuric acid. This traps heat, causing temperatures up to 880°F (471°C). Visiting spacecraft can only survive for a few hours.

FEATURES

- **Rotation**—Venus spins in the opposite direction to most planets. Plus, a day on Venus is longer than its year!

- **Atmosphere**—Studying the crushing pressure of Venus's atmosphere prompted scientists to look for an ozone hole on Earth. They found one, and then successfully worked to close it.

- **Volcanoes**—Venus has at least 1,600 volcanoes, but scientists don't know if they're still active.

MISSIONS

Mariner 2 flew past Venus in 1962, which made it the first spacecraft to visit another planet. DAVINCI+ and VERITAS (NASA/ESA) hope to launch at the end of the decade to study potential early forms of life on Venus.

SPACECRAFT SLINGSHOT

As a craft approaches a planet, it is pulled in by its gravity and then swung back out in a new direction. This is called a "gravitational slingshot." It is used to help spacecraft change their direction and speed as well as to save fuel.

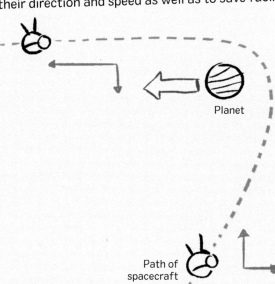

Planet

Path of spacecraft

JUPITER

This gas giant is currently hosting the JUNO spacecraft, which is studying its gravity and magnetic fields, answering key questions about how the solar system began. China aims to send a craft to Jupiter in the late 2020s.

COMETS & ASTEROIDS

Asteroids are large rocky leftovers from the formation of the solar system. They range in size from 30 ft. (10 m) across up to a colossal 300 mi. (500 km) wide. Asteroids show us what the solar system was like billions of years ago. On the other hand, comets are objects made of ice and dust that come from the colder far-flung edges of our solar system.

COMETS

Comets are large space snowballs made of ice, frozen gases, dust, and rock. As they move close to the Sun, they heat up and their gases start to thaw. This gives the comet a glowing head and the iconic "tail" of gases streaming away from the Sun. These can sometimes be seen with the naked eye.

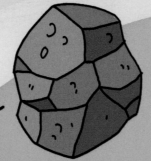

Asteroid—A rocky object mostly found in the asteroid belt, which is between Mars and Jupiter.

WHAT'S IN A NAME?

The name used for a chunk of space rock varies depending on where it is in space or Earth's atmosphere.

Meteoroid—A small chunk of rock that has broken away from an asteroid or comet.

Meteor—When a meteoroid enters Earth's atmosphere, it heats up and is vaporized as it shoots across the sky. Meteors are also known as shooting stars.

Meteorite—If a meteoroid survives the journey through Earth's atmosphere and impacts with Earth, it is called a meteorite.

WILLIAM AND CAROLINE HERSCHEL

William and Caroline Herschel were born Germany. In 1766 William moved to the U.K. to become a professional musician, and his sister Caroline performed in his concerts. However, both of them also developed a love of astronomy. William discovered the planet Uranus and detected infrared radiation from the Sun. Caroline discovered eight comets, a galaxy, and three nebulas, and she was the first woman ever to earn a living from astronomy. Together they discovered 2,400 astronomical objects.

METEOR SHOWERS

A meteor shower is when a number of meteors appear together, streaking the night sky with light. There are a few annual meteor showers that you won't want to miss. The Perseid meteor shower occurs every August in the Northern Hemisphere. In the Southern Hemisphere, keep an eye out for the Eta Aquarids in May.

ORBITING A COMET

In 2004, ESA's Rosetta became the the first spacecraft ever to orbit a comet, after making a ten-year journey to get there. The Rosetta craft mapped the comet and released a small lander named Philae, which landed successfully on the comet's bumpy surface.

STARS & GALAXIES

Scientists categorize stars based on their size, the different types of light they emit (their spectra), and their temperature. The Sun is the biggest object in our solar system, but it's pretty small compared with other stars. Like humans, stars and galaxies are born, they age, and their life has an end. They come in a range of shapes and sizes—here are a few of them.

Nebulas: These giant clouds of dust and gas can collapse because of gravity. This collapse puts the gas and dust under huge amounts of pressure, forming new stars.

Dwarf stars: Red dwarfs are the most common stars in the Milky Way. They're smaller than our Sun (a yellow dwarf) and therefore burn at a lower temperature. Red dwarfs are too dim for us to see from Earth.

Supernovas: Supergiants go out with a bang! Their life cycle ends as a powerful explosion called a supernova.

Supergiants: These are the brightest and most massive stars in the universe. They are created when a big star is in the final stages of its life cycle.

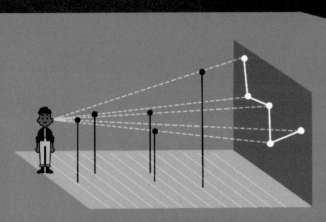

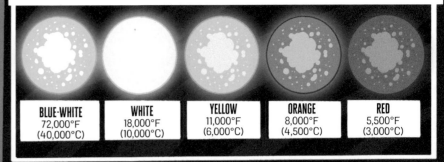

BLUE-WHITE	WHITE	YELLOW	ORANGE	RED
72,000°F (40,000°C)	18,000°F (10,000°C)	11,000°F (6,000°C)	8,000°F (4,500°C)	5,500°F (3,000°C)

CONSTELLATIONS

Stars can form patterns in the night sky, which we call constellations. From Earth, the stars in constellations appear to be next to each other, but actually they can be millions of light-years apart.

Pulsars: These stars are like lighthouses in the sky. They spin at a regular rate, sending out a beam of radiation that points toward Earth periodically.

GALAXIES

Like most things in life, galaxies come in all shapes and sizes. There are three main groups: spiral, elliptical, and irregular. Astronomers use telescopes on the ground and in space to better understand how galaxies form.

Halo
A surrounding sphere of lightly scattered stars, dust, and tightly packed regions of stars called globular clusters.

Spiral arm
Swirling regions where stars are formed. Young star clusters appear blue in color.

Central bulge
This area contains a high concentration of older stars and possibly a supermassive black hole.

Spiral galaxies: These galaxies are shaped like a disk, with several arms curving our from the center.

Elliptical galaxies: These galaxies are oval in shape. They contain little gas or dust so are home to old stars—they don't have the fuel to make new ones.

Irregular galaxies: Some galaxies don't have a shape but appear as a scattering of stars and gas. They contain old and young stars and can vary in size and brightness.

BEYOND OUR SOLAR SYSTEM

The area beyond our solar system is known as "interstellar space." With current technology, it would take us tens to hundreds of years to send missions this far. Sometimes we get lucky and an interstellar object visits us. Other times, scientists use instruments based on Earth to investigate other stellar neighborhoods.

INTERSTELLAR OBJECTS

Beyond our solar system there are asteroids that aren't bound to any star. 'Oumuamua was discovered in 2017, and became the first known interstellar traveller to pass through our solar system. It's thought to be hundreds of millions of years old and shaped like a sausage.

VOYAGER

No spacecraft has traveled farther than Voyagers 1 and 2, which launched in 1977. Voyager 1 transformed our understanding of Jupiter. Voyager 2 was the first probe to visit Uranus up close. In 2012 Voyager 1 crossed into interstellar space, becoming the first human-made object to do so, and Voyager 2 followed in 2018.

STEPHEN HAWKING (1942–2018)

Stephen Hawking was a British physicist and author who used mathematical models to figure out how the universe works. From an early age, he had a strong sense of wonder about the world around him, which led him to studying cosmology. At age 21, while studying at the University of Cambridge in the U.K., he was diagnosed with a disease that causes loss of muscle and nerve control. This didn't stop him from becoming one of the most iconic scientists of recent times. From black holes to the big bang, Hawking transformed our understanding of some of the biggest mysteries of the universe and wrote books that made science accessible to everyone.

EXOPLANETS

Planets outside of our solar system are called "exoplanets." The first one was detected in the 1990s, but over 5,000 planets have been confirmed to orbit other stars. The closest one is called Proxima Centauri B, and it would take 6,300 years to reach it.

THE GOLDILOCKS ZONE

Astronomers are constantly looking for exoplanets with water on the surface. To support life, they can't be too hot or too cold—they need to be "just right."

EXTRATERRESTRIALS

The organization SETI—the Search for Extraterrestrial Intelligence—is trying to understand the age-old question of whether we are alone in the universe. They search for proof of intelligent beings in other star systems.

BLACK HOLES

Astronomers believe there is a black hole in the center of large galaxies, including the Milky Way. They detect black holes by studying the influence they have on stars and gas nearby.

THE INTERNATIONAL SPACE STATION

The International Space Station (ISS) is an Earth-orbiting research lab, and it's the place astronauts call home during their time in space. The ISS was built in space, piece by piece, starting in 1998 and is now used by countries and organizations from all over the world. It travels at 5 mi. (8 km) per second and helps humans learn how to live and work in space. A lot of the science that happens on board the ISS couldn't be done anywhere else. Science experiments on the ISS teach us about life in space as well as helping us down on Earth.

Circling Earth

The ISS completes one lap of our planet every 90 minutes. It's the third-brightest object in the night sky and can be spotted with the naked eye. You can find out online when it will pass over your home.

Solar panels

The solar panels on the ISS use the Sun's energy to power the station. They are 358 ft. (109 m) long—that's longer than the world's largest passenger aircraft, and even longer than a football field!

Light pollution

City lights can appear brighter than stars from the ISS. Astronauts have teamed up with citizen scientists to monitor the light pollution that can impact life on our planet, from changes in bird migration to flowering times for plants.

Natural Disaster Response

The ISS can report if power has been restored to areas impacted by natural disaster. The Lightning Imaging Sensor aims to improve severe weather forecasting from space.

Space walks

Sometimes astronauts need to venture outside to repair parts of the space station. These trips are called space walks. There are robotic arms on the outside of the ISS that help astronauts move around.

Water purification

Astronauts on the ISS recycle 93% of their water. The same device used to recycle their water has helped communities on Earth, giving them access to clean water.

In and out

Docking ports allow spacecraft carrying supplies to connect to the ISS. When they need to go on a space walk, astronauts can leave through air locks, which open to the outside.

Living in space

The ISS is home to seven astronauts at a time, with six sleeping areas, two bathrooms, and a gym. It has the universe's best view of Earth, with a 360° window.

Growing Food

The ISS has its own greenhouse. Astronauts use it to grow plants, to see if fresh food could help sustain crew members on future long-duration flights.

ASTRONAUT

The term "astronaut" comes from the Greek words for star and sailor. It's a dream job for many people, but living in space is very different from life on Earth. Before they blast off, astronauts go through years of intense training and preparation. Plus, everything they need to survive is packed up with them. Space suits are different from your everyday clothes. Each suit is like a life-support bubble that keeps an astronaut safe while they are on a space walk or on the Moon.

DID YOU KNOW?
NASA designed boots for astronauts with ventilation and padding. Sports companies used this design to create cushioned shoe insoles for running.

Cameras and **lights** can be attached to an astronaut's helmet. This allows videos to be sent back down to Earth.

A space suit **helmet** is essential for breathing in space. It connects to an astronaut's ventilation system. It also has a visor, which protects the astronaut's eyes from the Sun's radiation and any dangerous space dust.

The **life-support system** has everything an astronaut could need: a fan, a water tank to keep the astronaut cool, a carbon dioxide removal system, electricity, and even a two-way radio! This is all packed into a high-tech backpack.

The hard **upper torso** is made from a similar material to some cars, called fiberglass. It's strong and connects the suit to the life-support system.

Astronauts wear **gloves** that contain heating elements so their fingers don't get too cold in space. This way, their hands aren't too stiff when they use tools outside the space station.

The **lower torso** protects the legs and feet. Suits are now more flexible in the lower half, so astronauts can walk rather than "hopping" like the Apollo astronauts. Different colored stripes are sometimes used to help identify individual astronauts.

THERE'S NO SPACE LIKE HOME

Living in space is different from everyday life. There are no stores in space, so astronauts bring supplies with them that need to last for months. They also use special equipment to keep their bodies fit and healthy while they're away from home.

ON EARTH

IN SPACE

Food: Space food is usually dehydrated and kept in pouches to keep it from spoiling. Astronauts simply add water and heat up their food. Because of weightlessness, the food won't fall off a fork or spoon and astronauts can eat in any direction, even upside down!

Exercise: Weightlessness looks fun, but it takes its toll on health. There's no gravity, which means your heart doesn't work as hard to pump blood around the body, and astronauts' bones can get weaker. To prevent too much damage, crew members strap themselves into exercise equipment and work out every day.

Showering: Most of the water on the ISS is recycled from the astronauts' breath, sweat, and urine! To wash their hair, astronauts use tiny amounts of water and shampoo that they don't wash out. They have to make sure water droplets don't float off and damage equipment.

Sleep: Sleep is important for everyone, including astronauts. But you won't find a typical bed in space. Instead, astronauts sleep in small cabins, with a sleeping bag attached to the wall. This keeps them from floating off and bumping into things.

TELESCOPES

The first telescope was invented in the Netherlands in 1608 for "seeing things far away as if they were nearby." Since then telescopes have become bigger and better, allowing us to see farther and farther into space. While most telescopes are based on the ground, there are a few positioned in space that capture the clearest images possible.

ON THE GROUND

Telescopes are often found high up in the mountains, far away from light pollution and where the atmosphere is thin. This allows astronomers to make clear observations of distant stars and galaxies.

United States
The Maunakea Observatory sits on top of a dormant volcano in Hawai'i. From radio to ultraviolet wavelengths, it has the clearest visibility on Earth. Maunakea was the first observatory to use computer-controlled telescopes.

United Kingdom
The powerful Lovell Telescope at Jodrell Bank isn't high up on a mountain. This large radio telescope captures signals in its bowl and reflects them to a focal point where the waves can be received.

China

FAST is a radio telescope in the Guizhou province of China. Its dish is a whopping 1,640 ft. (500 m) across, making it the world's largest single dish radio telescope.

India

The Indian Astronomical Observatory is located 14,800 ft. (4,500 m) up in the western Himalayas, making it one of the highest observatories in the world. Its telescopes work in the optical, infrared and gamma-ray parts of the spectrum.

IN SPACE

It can be hard to see faint objects from the ground, and Earth's atmosphere can blur images. Placing telescopes in space allows astronomers to avoid these problems.

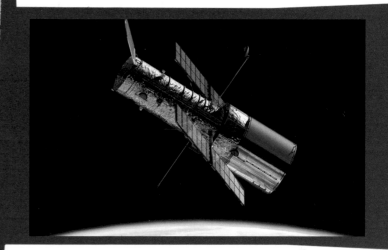

The Hubble Space Telescope

Launched in 1990, the Hubble Space Telescope has transformed how we see the universe and uncovered mysteries that we never knew existed. It not only views objects in visible light but also ultraviolet and infrared. It travels around Earth every 95 minutes and is close enough that astronauts have been able to repair it over the years.

The James Webb Space Telescope

Launched in December 2021, the James Webb Space Telescope is six times bigger than Hubble but half the weight. It's an infrared telescope, which allows it to look through clouds of dust and see the earliest stars in the universe. It was designed to be folded up inside a rocket and then to unfold in space after its launch.

SATELLITES

A satellite is something that orbits our planet. For example, the Moon is a natural satellite. We use artificial satellites every day to communicate and navigate, and also to monitor our world. These marvelous machines are carefully designed to travel at certain speeds and distances that balance with Earth's gravity. This means they stay in orbit and don't fly out into space.

SATELLITE POSITIONING

There are up to 5,000 satellites in orbit today. They travel in one of two directions. **Polar orbits** work from north to south and circle the entire globe twice in 24 hours. **Geostationary orbits** are farther out. These satellites move at the same rate as Earth so that they stay above the same location.

POLAR ORBIT

HIGH	MEDIUM	LOW
22,200 mi. (68,800 km)	12,645 mi. (160 km)	100 mi. (160 km)

GEOSTATIONARY ORBIT

SPACE JUNK

It's estimated that roughly 9,000 satellites have been launched since the very first one in 1957. But what goes up doesn't always come down. Old spacecraft, satellites, and stages of rockets are building up as space junk. This is a serious problem, and scientists are creating innovative ways to clean up space.

HOW THEY WORK

Satellites have a power source (usually a battery or solar panels) and an antenna. The antenna can send or receive radio waves to and from Earth. TV stations send their programs all around the world using radio waves that are transmitted by satellites.

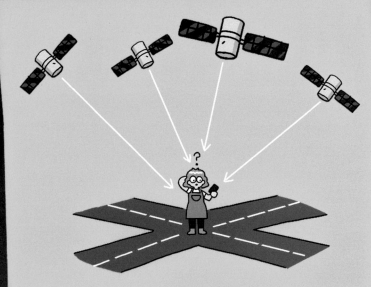

GLOBAL POSITIONING

Satellite navigation relies on at least four satellites sending signals toward Earth which are received by your phone or car navigation system. These receivers measure the time and distance taken for each signal to be sent from the satellites and use this to calculate where you are. This is what we call GPS, or the Global Positioning System.

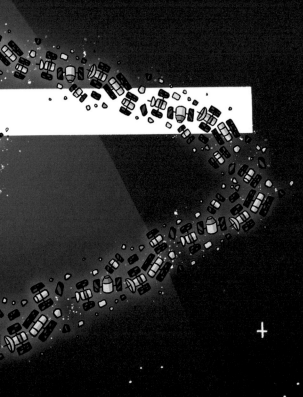

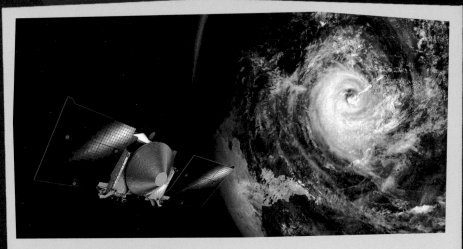

WEATHER SATELLITES

Scientists also use satellites to study Earth. Satellites can scan large areas and build up a picture of changes on Earth that are hard to see from the ground. This includes monitoring storms, melting glaciers, and disappearing coral reefs.

ROCKET SCIENCE

You can't have a mission to space without rockets! The main aims for a successful launch are to get the rocket moving, overcome Earth's gravity, and stay on the planned course. Rocket designs have changed over the years, but the science behind a rocket launch is still the same.

HOW IT WORKS

Fireworks and rockets both work using combustion—a chemical reaction in which fuel and an oxidizer burn, sending them whooshing into the air.

When the fuel and oxidizer burn, the rocket throws out exhaust very quickly, with a huge amount of force. The rocket thrusts into the air in the opposite direction to the exhaust, with the same amount of force. There are two main types of rockets, one fueled by liquid and the other by solid propellant.

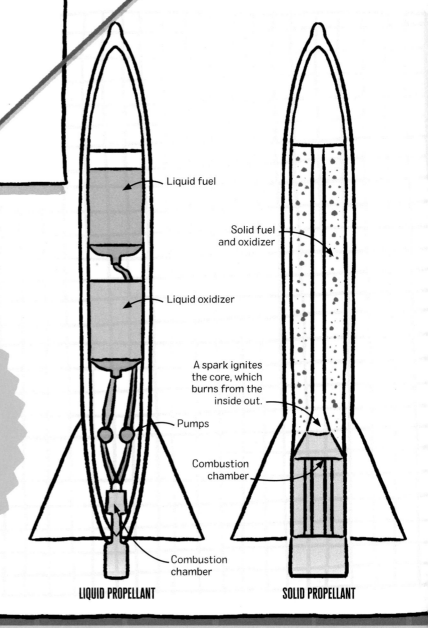

Liquid fuel

Solid fuel and oxidizer

Liquid oxidizer

A spark ignites the core, which burns from the inside out.

Pumps

Combustion chamber

Combustion chamber

LIQUID PROPELLANT

SOLID PROPELLANT

THE SPACE RACE

This time line shows what happened as the U.S. and U.S.S.R. raced to reach the Moon.

OCTOBER 4, 1957
The U.S.S.R. launches the first satellite, Sputnik 1.

NOVEMBER 3, 1957
The U.S.S.R. launches Sputnik 2, sending the first living animal into orbit—Laika the dog.

JANUARY 31, 1958
The U.S. launches its first satellite, Explorer 1.

AUGUST 19, 1960
In the U.S.S.R. Sputnik 5 completes the first return journey from space. It carries two dogs and some plants.

JANUARY 31, 1961
The U.S. sends Ham the chimpanzee into space, and he returns safely to Earth.

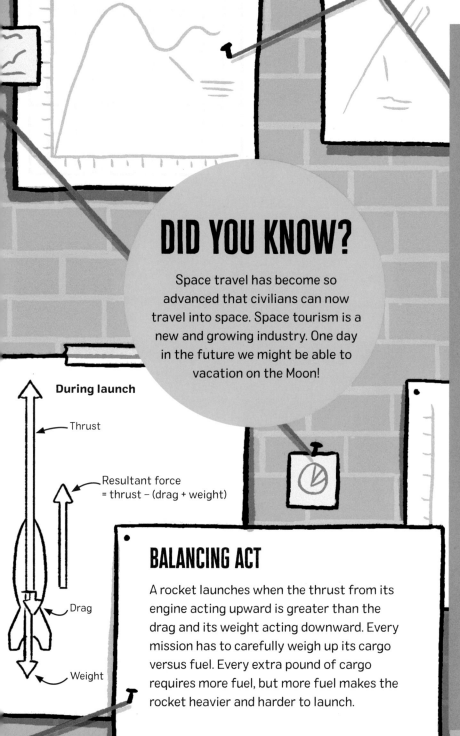

During launch

Thrust

Resultant force = thrust − (drag + weight)

Drag

Weight

BALANCING ACT

A rocket launches when the thrust from its engine acting upward is greater than the drag and its weight acting downward. Every mission has to carefully weigh up its cargo versus fuel. Every extra pound of cargo requires more fuel, but more fuel makes the rocket heavier and harder to launch.

MAE JEMISON (1956–)

Mae Jemison is an engineer, doctor, and former NASA astronaut. She attended Stanford University at the age of 16. After completing a degree in chemical engineering, Jemison attended Cornell University to become a doctor. In 1987 she was one of the 15 applicants out of 2,000 to be accepted onto NASA's astronaut training program. In 1992 Jemison became the first black woman to go into space, on board the space shuttle *Endeavour*.

APRIL 12, 1961
U.S.S.R. cosmonaut Yuri Gagarin becomes the first person in space, on Vostok 1.

MAY 5, 1961
Alan Shepard makes the first pilot-controlled journey and becomes the first American in space.

JUNE 16, 1963
U.S.S.R. cosmonaut Valentina Tereshkova becomes the first civilian and first woman in space.

MARCH 18, 1965
U.S.S.R. cosmonaut Alexei Leonov completes the first space walk.

DECEMBER 21, 1968
U.S. spacecraft Apollo 8 carries the first human crew in orbit around the Moon and returns to Earth.

JULY 20, 1969
U.S. spacecraft Apollo 11 lands the first humans on the Moon—Neil Armstrong and Edwin "Buzz" Aldrin. They return safely to Earth.

SUN SHIELDS

We all love to feel the sun's rays on our face, but we have to be careful. The Sun is 93 million mi. (150 million km) away, but its radiation can still damage us—we use sunscreen and parasols to stay protected. We're not the only things that need to be careful of the Sun's radiation. Scientists have spent decades creating the perfect materials to protect spacecraft from our neighborhood star's heat and radiation. But how do they work?

FEELING HOT, HOT, HOT!

The James Webb Space Telescope will be looking for heat signals from the first stars in the universe. To do this, it needs to stay really cold. It has a huge, shiny sun shield with five layers of a material called Kapton, which doesn't melt or burn. Each layer is also coated in aluminum. The layers block the Sun's heat and reflect it back into space.

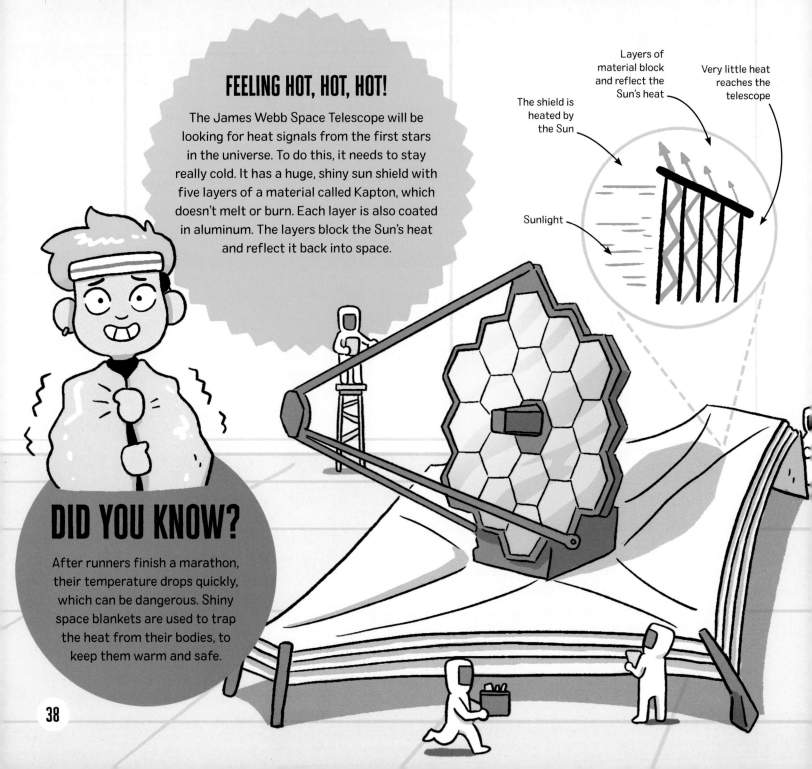

Layers of material block and reflect the Sun's heat

Very little heat reaches the telescope

The shield is heated by the Sun

Sunlight

DID YOU KNOW?

After runners finish a marathon, their temperature drops quickly, which can be dangerous. Shiny space blankets are used to trap the heat from their bodies, to keep them warm and safe.

THE HARVARD COMPUTERS

The Harvard Computers were a team of women who made an enormous contribution to astronomy from the late 1870s to the mid 1920s. Without any formal training, they combed through hundreds of thousands of glass-plated images of tens of millions of stars. It was their job to catalog these stellar objects. In doing so, they discovered how to calculate the distance from Earth to the stars, and they created a way to identify different types of stars, which we still use today.

THE SOLAR ORBITER

ESA-NASA's Solar Orbiter is taking the closest images of the Sun ever captured. It needs to survive intense radiation and heat that is 13 times stronger than on Earth. The orbiter's heat shield is covered in a charcoal-like powder called calcium phosphate, which absorbs the heat. The calcium phosphate is followed by 18 layers of titanium foil to keep any heat away from the equipment.

BLOCKING THE LIGHT

Have you ever worn a baseball cap on a sunny day? It creates shade and blocks out light so you can see. The space equivalent of this is called a coronagraph. It's an instrument that blocks the light from distant stars to help astronomers study planets that are orbiting nearby.

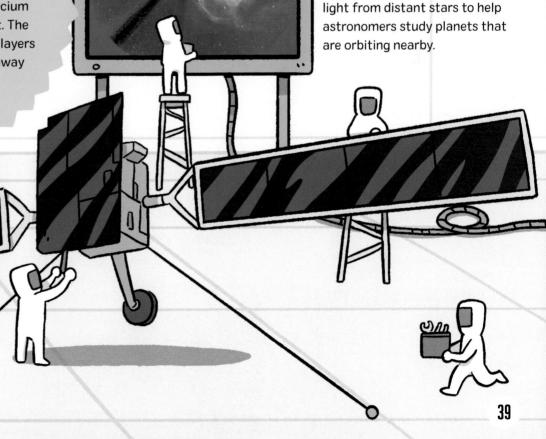

Planet

RETURNING ROCKETS

There's no doubt that rockets are awesome, but there are two big problems with them: they can usually only be used once, and they're really expensive to make. Luckily, we are constantly learning how to do things better, and we now have rockets that can launch, return to Earth, and be reused. This saves money and stops us from leaving junk out in space. These diagrams show how two different types of reusable rockets work.

BLUE ORIGIN

Blue Origin has a small capsule on top that separates from the rocket. The main body of the rocket returns to land. The capsule enters free flight and returns to land separately, using parachutes.

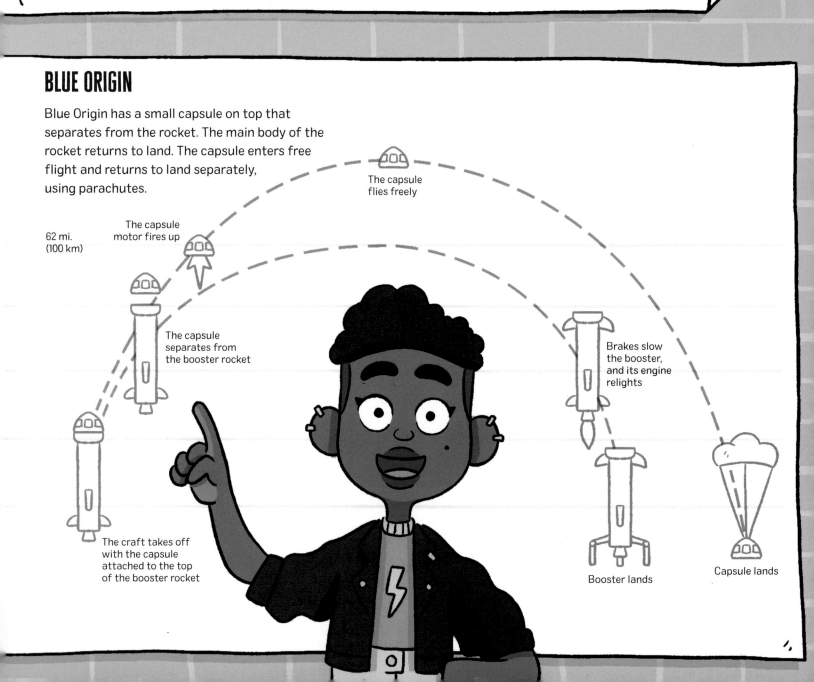

The capsule flies freely

62 mi. (100 km)

The capsule motor fires up

The capsule separates from the booster rocket

Brakes slow the booster, and its engine relights

The craft takes off with the capsule attached to the top of the booster rocket

Booster lands

Capsule lands

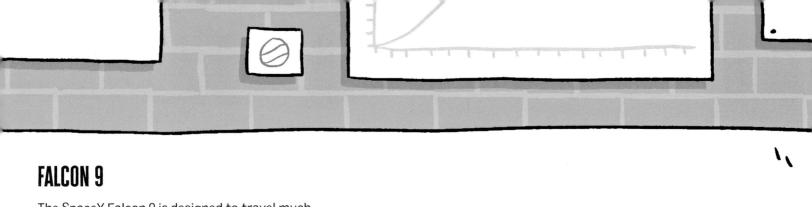

FALCON 9

The SpaceX Falcon 9 is designed to travel much farther into space than Blue Origin. The first stage is designed to land back on Earth, while its payload could reach the International Space Station.

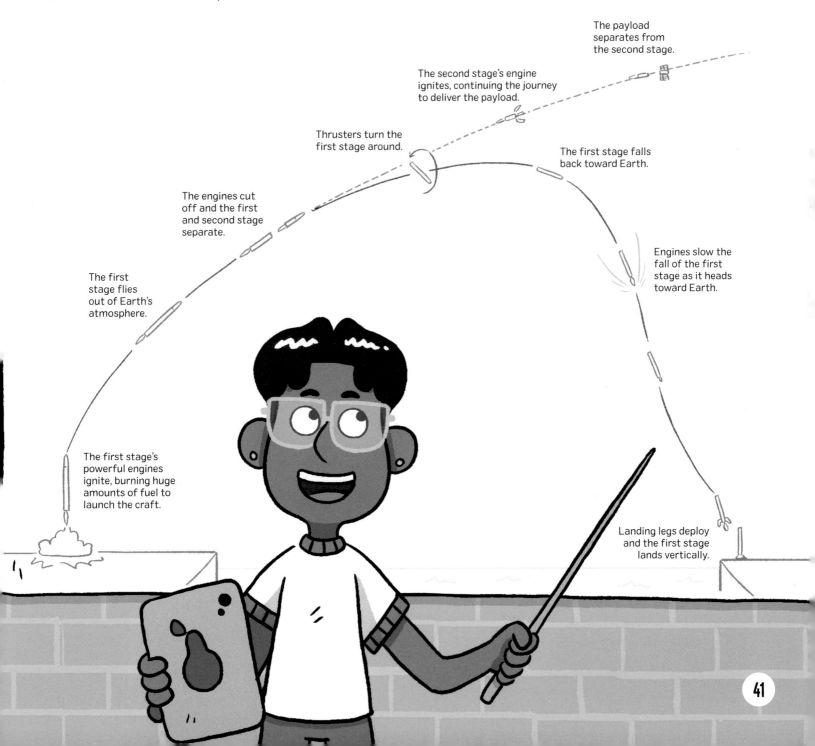

The payload separates from the second stage.

The second stage's engine ignites, continuing the journey to deliver the payload.

Thrusters turn the first stage around.

The first stage falls back toward Earth.

The engines cut off and the first and second stage separate.

The first stage flies out of Earth's atmosphere.

Engines slow the fall of the first stage as it heads toward Earth.

The first stage's powerful engines ignite, burning huge amounts of fuel to launch the craft.

Landing legs deploy and the first stage lands vertically.

ROCKET TEA

Is it a bird? Is it a plane? Is it a . . . tea bag? Building your own rocket doesn't have to be difficult. All you need are some things from the kitchen and you'll be taking to the skies in no time.

YOUR TURN!

WARNING:
Have an adult supervise!

INSTRUCTIONS

1. Cut off the top of the tea bag, removing any staples or string. Empty the leaves into a mug or the trash can.

2. Find yourself a safe, open area. Open up the tea bag so that it looks like a tube, and stand it on the plate. Make sure you have an adult with you.

3. With an adult watching, light the top edge of the tea bag so that it catches fire.

4. Lift off!

1

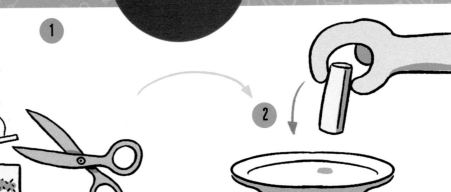

2

3

4

WHAT'S GOING ON?

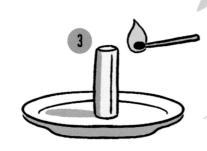

As the tube burns, it creates a current of hot air moving upward. As the hot air moves up, cold air rushes in to replace it. This convection current creates enough force for the tea bag to lift up and off the plate.

ANTIGRAVITY CHOCOLATE

Gravity is amazing—it stops us (and our chocolate) from drifting off into space. But what if you could make chocolate float just a little bit? This experiment shows you how. It's not magic—it's physics!

YOUR TURN!

YOU WILL NEED
- Chocolate-covered malt balls
- A glass that's narrower at the top than at the bottom, such as a wine glass

INSTRUCTIONS

1. Put a malt ball on the table and place the glass over it. Don't eat it!

2. Quickly move the glass in a circular motion, and watch the malt ball climb up the inside of the glass.

3. Still moving, lift the glass off the table. The malt ball should stay on the inside.

WHAT'S GOING ON?

The glass exerts an inward force on the malt ball, making it travel in a circle rather than in a straight line. The curve of the glass means the ball is pushed upward, and the glass supports its weight.

SOUND VACUUM

In space, you wouldn't hear a bell ring because it's a vacuum (there's no air). However, you would have to travel a long way to prove that! Instead, why not try creating your own vacuum at home?

YOUR TURN!

YOU WILL NEED
- Small bell
- Pipe cleaner
- Vacuum pump and stopper
- Clear glass bottle

INSTRUCTIONS

1. Attach one end of the pipe cleaner to the bell and the other end to the bottom of the wine stopper.

2. Lower the bell into the bottle and push the stopper into bottle's opening. Make sure the bell can't hit the side of the glass. At this point, you should still be able to hear the bell.

3. Use the vacuum pump to remove as much air as possible. What happens when you ring the bell now? Silence!

WHAT'S GOING ON?
Sound travels as vibrations in the air. When the air is removed from the bottle, a vacuum is created. Without air, sound can't travel—just like in space.

STARGAZING

Look up! You don't have to jump on a rocket to explore the wonders of space. You can see planets, stars, and even different galaxies just by stepping outside. You could even use a smartphone to photograph night-sky objects.

YOUR TURN!

YOU WILL NEED
- A clear night sky!
- Warm clothes if you're heading outside
- Snacks and a warm drink
- A smartphone
- For a better view, bring binoculars or a telescope

INSTRUCTIONS
- Stand away from any lights—this will let your eyes adjust to the darkness.
- Turn off the blue light on your smartphone and put it in "red mode" or "night shift."
- Align the phone's camera with the binoculars.

Sea of Cold
Plato Crater
Sea of Rains
Copernicus Crater
Kepler Crater
Ocean of Storms

Sea of Serenity
Sea of Crises
Sea of Tranquility
Stevinus Crater
Tycho Crater

The near side of the Moon

WHAT CAN YOU SEE?
- Can you see a satellite? They appear as small lights moving very slowly and uniformly.
- Which constellations can you see?
- What is the phase of the Moon?
- What features of the Moon can you see? This image is labeled with the names of some of them.

GLOSSARY

Airlock
A small room that is used for moving between areas with different air pressure, such as between the ISS and space outside.

Asteroid
A large space rock left over from when the solar system formed.

Atmosphere
The layer of gases surrounding Earth, held in place by gravity.

Atom
The smallest component of matter.

Axis
An imaginary line through an object, such as a planet, around which it spins.

Citizen scientists
Ordinary people taking part in scientific research, for example by observing the night sky or wildlife.

Comet
An object made of ice, frozen gases, dust, and rock that travels through the cold, faraway regions of our solar system, trailing a glowing tail of gas behind it.

Cosmology
The study of how the Universe began.

Crater
A bowl shaped dip on the surface of a planet or moon.

Element
A substance that cannot be broken down into another substance. Each element has its own type of atom.

Galaxies
Huge collections of billions of stars.

Gravity
The force pulling objects toward each other or down to the ground.

Light year
The distance that light travels in a year.

Magnetic field
The area surrounding a magnet or magnetic object (such as Earth), where the magnetic force acts.

Mass
The amount of matter—or stuff—something is made of.

Meteoroid
A lump of space rock that has broken away from an asteroid or comet. If it enters Earth's atmosphere, it is called a **meteor**. Then if it lands on Earth it is called a **meteorite**.

NASA
National Aeronautics and Space Administration—the U.S. space agency.

Orbit
To travel around something, pulled by gravity. A planet orbits the stars, for example. The path an object takes as it travels round is also called its orbit.

Payload
The thing being carried by a rocket.

Radiation
Rays of energy. Light, X-rays and microwaves are some types of radiation.

Thesis
A long piece of academic writing.

Universe
Everything that exists—all of space and everything in it.

U.S.S.R.
A huge country that spread throughout Europe and Asia in the 20th century, made up of Russia and many other countries.

Vacuum
Completely empty space. A vacuum contains no matter at all.

Picture credits
The Publisher would like to thank the following for permission to reproduce their material.
Top = t; Bottom = b; Center = c; Left = l; Right = r
5t Planck Collaboration/European Space Agency/Science Photo Library, 5b Volker Sringel/
Max Planck Institute for Astrophysics/Science Photo Library; 9r ESA/Hubble/NASA/Science
Photo Library; 10tl NASA Images; 12l NASA Goddard Space Flight Center/Science Photo Library,
12c David Parker/Science Photo Library, 12ct Portra/iStock Images, 12br petesphotography/iStock
Images; 13tl Just_Super/iStock Images, 13b NASA Images, 13tc NASA Images, 13r Gwengoat/iStock
Images; 19bl NASA Images; 20bl NASA Images; 24tc and 24br NASA Images, 24bl European Southern
Observatory/Science Photo Library; 25bl , 25br and 25cr NASA Images; 29 all NASA Images; 32bl Bob
London / Alamy Stock Photo, 32br tonystamp11/iStock Images; 33tr and 33br NASA Images, 33tl
Imaginechina Limited / Alamy Stock Photo, 33br beibaoke / Alamy Stock Photo; 35bl Elen11/iStock
Images; 39c NASA/Science Photo Library; 45b Onfokus/iStock Images.

INDEX

THE AUTHOR & ILLUSTRATOR

IZZIE CLARKE

Izzie Clarke is a science journalist, author, and award-winning podcast producer. Combining a master's degree in physics with a background in entertainment radio, she has tried astronaut training, race-car driving, and making fireworks in her mission to show young people the exciting world of science. Izzie hosts "The Supermassive Podcast" for the Royal Astronomical Society in the U.K., was a broadcaster/producer for BBC 5 Live Science, and is currently enjoying the adventure of writing her first books.

JAMES LANCETT

James is a Bath, England–based illustrator, director, and yellow sock lover! As a child he was obsessed with cartoons, video games, and fantasy. As he grew up and became more beardy, these inspirations held strong and he moved to London to study illustration and animation at Kingston University. His degree opened the door to the job James had always dreamed of—he now works as an illustrator, storyboard artist, and animation director.